P9-BIT-590

Mom

Compiled and Written by Rhonda S. Hogan

Illustrated by Judy Buswell

Brownlow

Little Treasures
Miniature Books

A Little Book of Love

A Little Cup of Tea

A Little Nest of Pleasant Thoughts

All Things Great & Small

All Things Grow With Love

Baby's First Little Book

Baby's First Little Book of Angels

Beside Still Waters • Catch of The Day

Dear Daughter • Dear Teacher

Faithful Friends • For My Secret Pal

Grandmothers Are for Loving

Happiness Is Homemade

Mom, I Love You

My Sister, My Friend

Quiet Moments of Inspiration

Quilted Hearts • Rose Petals

Seasons of Friendship

Soft As the Voice of an Angel

Tea Time Friends • They Call It Golf

For some, mother is a homemaker who is always there to soothe hurt feelings or bandage a scraped knee. For others, mother is a breadwinner who goes off to work each morning, and comes home at night with eager anticipation. But for most of us, mother is someone who is a constant in a sea of change. She teaches us about life and love. She is the one who makes daily

sacrifices as we grow, who helps us as
we take our first faltering steps as
a child and then as a young adult.
Through her endless patience and love we
in turn learn not only to love ourselves
at our most awkward moments, but to
love others as well. It is this love that
can only be passed down from mother
to child, generation after generation.

R.S.H.

What is a home
without a mother?

ALICE HAWTHORNE

Many women
have done excellently,
but you surpass them all.

PROVERBS 31:29

Dear Mom,

I want you to know how special you are to me,
You've filled my life with love and sincerity.
From my first step
To my high school graduation
You've always been there
Without hesitation.
You've picked me up
When life got me down.
You've guided me
Without uttering a sound.
My life has been blessed
Because of you—
I can't thank you enough, Mom,
For all that you do.

TAMMY RICHERSON

My mother was the source
from which I derived
the guiding principles of my life.

JOHN WESLEY

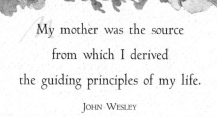

No nation ever had a better friend
than the mother who taught
her children to pray.

ANONYMOUS

Children, like roses,

always thrive on love

R.S.H.

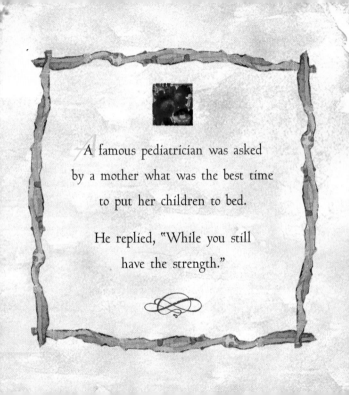

A famous pediatrician was asked
by a mother what was the best time
to put her children to bed.

He replied, "While you still
have the strength."

My mother believed
in saving the best for last,
and getting all the work done
before having fun. Her conviction
to this principle was so thorough
that even when eating watermelon,
she always saved the best bite
for last.

P.C.B.

Judy Buswell

Like a Rose

A mother's love is like
a rose—always blooming,
forever caring, always giving,
forever sharing.

R.S.H.

Home should be a retreat to which
a son or daughter can return in triumph or
defeat, in victory or disgrace, and know
they will be loved.

ANONYMOUS

She is clothed with strength and dignity;

she can laugh at the days to come.

Her children arise and call her blessed;

her husband also, and he praises her:

"Many women do noble things,

but you surpass them all."

PROVERBS 31:25, 28-29

Judy Burnett

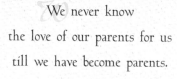

We never know
the love of our parents for us
till we have become parents.

HENRY WARD BEECHER

Elephants and grandchildren
never forget.

ANONYMOUS

And wherever we may turn
This lesson we shall learn
A boy's best friend is his mother.

JOSEPH P. SKELLEY

Something has been discovered
that does the work
of five men—one mother.

There is no higher height
to which humanity can attain
than that occupied
by a devoted,
heaven-inspired,
praying mother.

ANONYMOUS

Only Then

It is only when you are grown-up
that you can truly appreciate your
mother. By stepping back from her
or leaving home for your own career
or your own home—it is only then
that you can measure her greatness
and fully appreciate it.

R.S.H.

A Gentle Kiss

My mother would sing songs

before I went to bed,

She would tuck my pillow gently

up under my head.

The sweet sounds of her voice

slowly put me to sleep,

As she placed a gentle kiss upon my cheek.

JoAnn Washington

A rich child often
sits in a poor mother's lap.

DANISH PROVERB

God has placed
the genius of women in their hearts,
because the works of this genius
are always works of love.

LAMARTINE

In a crowded mall a little boy
lost his mother. He went in and out
of stores and saw women carrying pack-
ages, but none was his mother. He finally
found a security guard and, pointing to
the passing crowd, asked, "Mister,
did you happen to see a woman
going by without me?"

JOHN R. BROKHOFF

A mother understands
what a child does not say.

JEWISH PROVERB

We cannot hold a torch
to light another's path
without brightening our own.

BEN SWEETLAND

Most mothers
are instinctive philosophers.

Harriet Beecher Stowe

In all my efforts to learn to read,
my mother shared fully my ambition
and sympathized with me and aided
me in every way she could.

Booker T. Washington

Youth is a gift of nature.

Age is a work of art.

ENGLISH PROVERB

Who takes the child by the hand,

takes the mother by the heart.

DANISH PROVERB

Now that my kids are grown
and gone and I have the phone
to myself, I can't remember who
I wanted to call.

PEGGY GOLDTRAP

No one is poor
who had a godly mother.

ABRAHAM LINCOLN

A man never sees all that his mother
has been to him until it is too late
to let her know that he sees it.

WILLIAM DEAN HOWELLS

Love is a great thing,
a good above all others,
which alone makes every burden light.

THOMAS A. KEMPIS

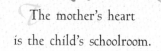

The mother's heart
is the child's schoolroom.

HENRY WARD BEECHER

Next to God we are indebted
to women, first for life itself,
and then for making it worth having.

BOVEE

I can still smell the freshly baked cookies and taste the big glass of cold milk that were always on the table waiting for me when I arrived home from a busy day at school. You were synonymous with June Cleaver on "Leave It to Beaver." You were always home when I got there. You made sure I had a freshly scrubbed look at all times, glistening hair,

and a starched dress. You saw to it that I had
music lessons the first twenty years of my life,
which taught me great self-discipline.
I look at you now with advanced Alzheimer's
disease and realize you are gone. You are not
my mother any longer but only the outer shell
of what once was. My hope for you is that
somewhere in your mind once in awhile
circuits connect and you, if only for a second,
realize that you are loved.

MARCI ISAACS

One of the most pleasant ways
to a mother's heart is through
the doors of a good restaurant.

ANONYMOUS

Is not a young mother one of the
sweetest sights life shows us?

WILLIAM M. THACKERAY

Moms teach us to do nearly everything.
But one of the most important is to
keep the sacred things of life sacred.

CAROLINE BROWNLOW

Children, keep your father's commands
and do not forsake your mother's teaching.
Bind them upon your heart forever.

PROVERBS 6:20

It is when we forget ourselves
that we do things
that will be remembered.

AUTHOR UNKNOWN

Youth fades, love droops,
The leaves of friendship fall;
A mother's secret hope
Outlives them all.

OLIVER WENDELL HOLMES

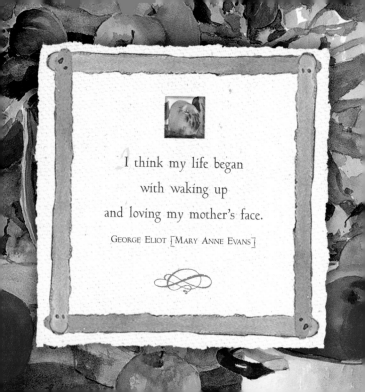

I think my life began
with waking up
and loving my mother's face.

GEORGE ELIOT [MARY ANNE EVANS]

If our love is always discrete and
calculating, never carried beyond itself,
it is not true love. Love is spontaneous;
it bursts out in extraordinary ways.

OSWALD CHAMBERS

God can do tremendous things
through people who don't care
who gets the credit.

ANONYMOUS

Name Two

A ten-year old boy left the table without finishing the wonderful lunch his mother had prepared for him. In exasperation she asked, "How could you leave so much of your food untouched? Don't you know millions of people around the world are starving to death?" The boy promptly replied, "Name two!"

Where there is a mother in the house,
matters speed well.

AMOS BRONSON ALCOTT

One of the hardest things
about rearing children is convincing them
that you have seniority.

ANONYMOUS

A Precious Gift

Children, look in those eyes,

listen to that dear voice,

notice the feeling of even a single touch

that is bestowed upon you

by that gentle hand! Make much of it

while yet you have that most precious

of all good gifts, a loving mother.

MACAULAY

Mother's Covers

When you were small
And just a touch away,
I covered you with blankets
Against the cool night air.

But now that you are tall
And out of reach,
I fold my hands
And cover you in prayer.

AUTHOR UNKNOWN